YOUNG PEOPLE'S STORY OF

OUR HERITAGE

YOUNG PEOPLE'S STORY OF OUR HERITAGE

ARCHITECTURE

by

V. M. HILLYER and E. G. HUEY

New Edition Designed and Revised by Childrens Press, Chicago

Consultants

Howard Dearstyne, Associate Professor of Architecture
Illinois Institute of Technology, Chicago, Illinois

H. F. Koeper, Associate Professor of Architecture
University of Illinois, Chicago Circle Campus, Chicago, Illinois

Meredith Press, New York

Illustrations in the order in which they appear

Library of Congress Catalog Card Number: 66-11326

Contents

Acknowledgments

Cover drawing: John Hollis—Hollis Associates.

Cover photograph: View of the Burg Katz in the Rhine Valley.
German Tourist Information Office, Chicago

Page 2: Castle Neuschwanstein, Fiessen, Germany.
Pan American Airways

Frontis: A minaret; the carved, slender, balconied tower of a mosque in Alexandria, Egypt.
Trans World Airlines Photo

Opposite: Carytid from the Porch of the Maidens, The Erechtheum, Athens.
Photo by Chan Forman

Designed by John Hollis

Edited by Joan Downing

ARCHITECTURE

3000 B.C.—Gothic Period

Egyptian Pyramids, the Oldest Houses in the World

A group of men in America were talking about houses when one of them asked me, "How old is your house?" "Five years old," I replied. "Well, my house is over a hundred years old," said the man. "It's in Massachusetts."

"Only a hundred years old!" exclaimed another man. "My house is two hundred years old. It's in Virginia."

"That doesn't seem old to me," still another man said. "My house is four hundred and fifty years old."

Each one was trying to tell a bigger story than the other.

"Four hundred and fifty years old!" I cried. "How can that be? That's before America was discovered!"

"It isn't in America," he replied. "It's in England. I'm an Englishman."

"Oh, well, that's different. If you count houses outside of America, I've been in a house that's a thousand years old. It's a church in France."

"Only a thousand years old?" The Englishman seemed bent on going me one better. "I've been in a house built two thousand years ago. It's in Greece—a temple. It is called the Parthenon."

"Well," said I, not to be outdone, "I can beat that. I've been in a house that is five thousand years old—a house built for the dead. It's in Egypt. It is a pyramid."

"You win," said the Englishman. "No one can beat that."

And that's true. The oldest houses in the world are the pyramids in Egypt—houses for the dead. But why are the oldest houses, houses for the dead? Where are the houses of the living—the houses built five thousand years ago to live in?

They're all gone—long, long ago—and the reason is this: A man expected to live only fifty years or so and he built his house out of wood or mud bricks to last only as long as he expected to live; so the wood houses have all rotted away and the houses made of mud brick have turned back to dust. But he expected to be a long time dead so if he were a king, he built a house for himself to be dead in, and he built it to last till judgment day.

You see, the Egyptians, hundreds of years before Christ, believed in resurrection. They believed their dead bodies would sometime come to life again, so they built the pyramids out of stone to last till then, and they had their bodies embalmed—that is, made into what we call mummies—to last till then also. The pyramids are still there in Egypt, but the mummies that were once in them are not in them any more. They have been stolen or have been taken away and put in museums—in museums for anyone and everyone to gaze upon, in spite of all the care that the tomb builder took to have his body undisturbed.

British Overseas Airways Corporation

One of the pyramids at
Gizeh, Cairo, Egypt

Over a hundred pyramids were built near the river Nile by Egypt's rulers, but the largest is one built by King Cheops about three thousand years before Christ was born—about five thousand years ago. The pyramid is almost five hundred feet high, even though the top has been broken off. It is by far the largest stone building in the world—a mountain of stone.

The pyramid of Cheops is built of solid rock on a natural rock foundation. Since there was no rock nearby for building the pyramid itself, it had to be brought from quarries. Some of these quarries were fifty miles away and some were five hundred miles away. Then it had to be

The Sphinx and the Pyramid of Cheops at Gizeh

Egyptian State Tourist Administration. Photo by C. Zachary.

dragged fifty miles or five hundred miles from the quarry. Some of the huge stones weighed more than a loaded freight car; it took years to drag the rocks to the site of the pyramid.

You see, there was no machinery in those days—no pulleys or derricks, no tracks or trucks, no engines or mechanical contrivances—such as we have today to lift and carry huge loads, so that every block of stone had to be pushed or pulled by sheer brute force. Hundreds of men tugged from in front and hundreds shoved from behind. And then each block had to be lifted and moved into place. Probably a roadway was built right up the side of the pyramid to where the block could be slid into position. It is supposed to have taken twenty years to build Cheops' pyramid and they say the king employed over a hundred thousand men to do the job.

The outside of the pyramid when it was finished was smooth, polished stone—perhaps in bands of different colored granite, but long ago all this covering of polished stone was stolen and carried off to make other buildings, so that the sides of the pyramid are now rough, irregular steps, each one several feet high; you can climb to the top on any side simply by climbing from one step to another.

The Great Pyramid, as we call it, if it were sliced through the center like a piece of cheese, would show three small rooms one above the other and some slanting passageways to the three rooms. The rest is solid rock.

The topmost room was for the king's own mummy. In order to make sure that the weight of the stone above would not crush through the room in which the mummy was, he had five ceilings of stone built, one above the other, with a space above each ceiling and then a slanting ceiling above them all. The two lines slanting upward from his room to the sides are small air passages. The room underneath his own was for his queen and the one under that, in the cellar or foundation of the pyramid, was perhaps for nobody. That was for awhile the great mystery of the Great Pyramid, but now we feel we have guessed the riddle. You see, there was only one passageway starting from the outside. From this one passageway another secret passageway led off to the king's and queen's chambers, but the passage that went straight ahead led down to the room that had nothing in it. Cheops was afraid that after he and his queen had been buried away in this tomb, some enemy of his might try to steal their mummies

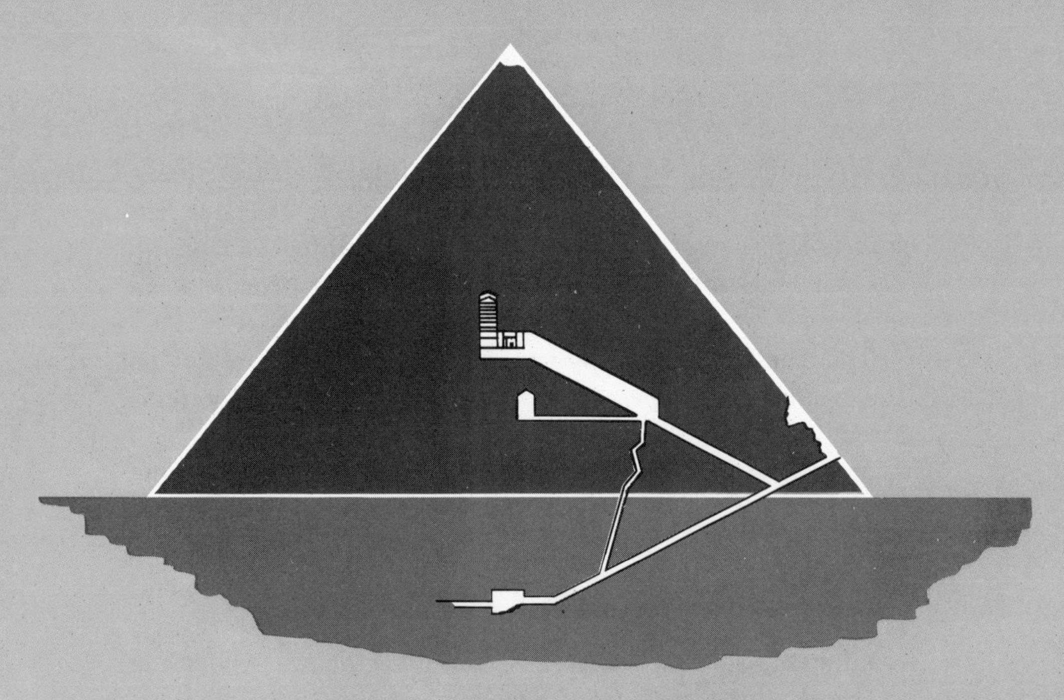

Cross section of the Great Pyramid

and so prevent them from coming to life again on judgment day. So he had all the passageways filled up with stone after he was buried, and then had the entrance covered so that no one could find where or how to get in.

But Cheops figured that if someone *did* find the entrance and began to dig out the passageway down to the cellar, this straight passage would lead off the track and he would keep digging down and not see the other secret passageway leading off to the king's and queen's chambers. Then when he did reach the empty room, he would find nothing.

But in spite of all these extraordinary precautions that Cheops took to prevent anyone's finding his mummy, all these passageways and rooms *were* later discovered and opened and the mummies were removed—to where or by whom, no one knows.

Though there are over a hundred pyramids, not all of them have the true pyramid form. That is, not all of them are triangular. In some pyramids the sides slope in very little at the bottom and then, as if the builder had changed his mind, they slope in faster toward the top. The Pharaoh who built his tomb like this may have been sick and afraid he was going to die before the pyramid was finished and so had to hurry up. In some of the pyramids the sides zigzag toward the top in several giant-like steps. Perhaps the Pharaoh just wanted to have his pyramid different from all the others. Some of the pyramids are built of brick instead of stone.

The three greatest pyramids stand close together on the sands of the desert in giant majesty as they have stood for ages past.

Mere size doesn't make a thing beautiful. A big thing may be very ugly. But the pyramids are monuments to man's attempt to make something enduring, lasting, and the builders succeeded in making the most permanent, lasting thing ever built by man. The pyramids are also monuments to their belief in a life after death. And when we think of the millions of people who have come and gone, lived and died, since these mighty monuments were built, and the countless millions who will come and go while the pyramids still stand on, it sets us thinking of the shortness of our lives and the awesome length of eternity.

All the pyramids were tombs, but not all tombs were pyramids. That is, some tombs were not pyramid-shaped at all, but just stone buildings with flat tops. Furthermore, some tombs were merely caves cut into the rock cliffs on the west side of the Nile. These rock tombs were hollowed out on the west side of the river so that the entrance would face east, toward the rising sun. The Egyptians never faced their tombs any other way, for they thought the sun god could not wake the dead on judgment day unless the tomb faced him as he rose in the east. If the tomb faced him he would wake these people who were dead, just as the rising sun shining into east windows wakes a sleeper in the morning.

A rock-cut tomb at Beni Hasan is particularly interesting because it has columns in front—columns cut out of the selfsame rock. None of the pyramid tombs had columns.

So these are the oldest houses in the world. Houses of the dead—pyramids and tombs.

---

right: Rock-cut tomb at Beni Hasan

Historical Pictures Service, Chicago

Temples for the Gods

Most of you at some time or another have built a house. It may have been a house of cards that blew over very easily, or it may have been made of books, or it may have been made of building blocks, or it may have been a shack in the back yard.

Now, every house must have walls and a roof. If you lean two blocks or cards together the walls form the roof and the roof forms the walls. That is the simplest way—the sides form both walls and roof, as in a tent or a wigwam. The sides of the pyramids were both walls and roof. A pyramid was shaped something like a tent, but was built solid except for the small rooms in the center.

I told you the oldest buildings were tombs. The next-oldest buildings were temples—houses men built for their gods. In England there is a ruin of what we once thought was a temple. It probably never had a roof, but you can see several stone crossbeams still in place. It is called Stonehenge. I am showing it to you here because the stones still standing show very well how it was built—not like the pyramids were built, but by putting one stone across two standing stones. This way of building is called *post and lintel.*

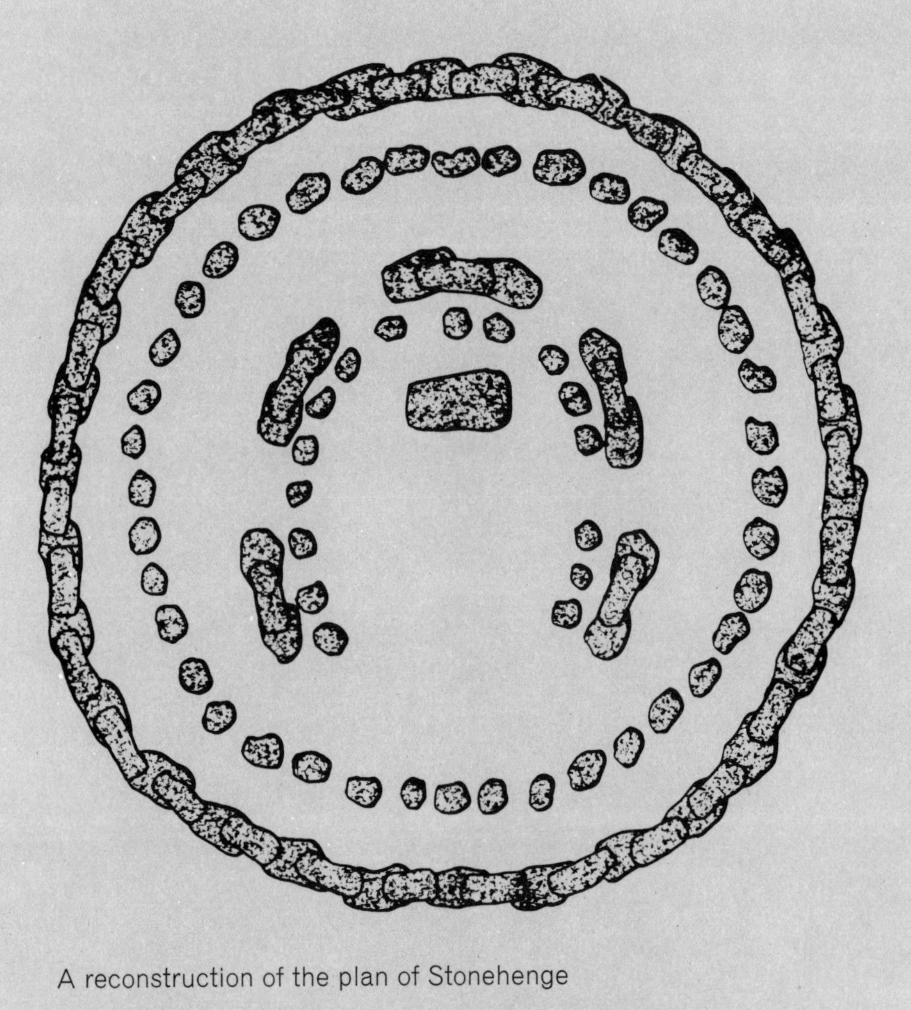

A reconstruction of the plan of Stonehenge

The ruins of Stonehenge look very much like something a child might build out of blocks—two blocks standing up with one laid across. But these blocks are of stone, immense stones many times larger than a man. Stonehenge may have been built to enclose a space that was set aside as holy ground, where the ancient men came to worship their sun god. Some people think that Stonehenge was built by Druids—members of an ancient religious order who lived in Gaul, Britain, and Ireland.

British Travel Association

Stonehenge,
on the
Salisbury Plain
near London

One of the greatest and oldest temples is in Egypt. It is the temple at Karnak, part of which was built by Rameses the Great, the Pharaoh who ordered all the Israelite children in Egypt killed. It also is a ruin and one of the most beautiful ruins in the world. You may feel that a ruin could not be beautiful. A broken-down and dilapidated house or man is not usually beautiful. Why do you suppose this ruin of Karnak is called beautiful?

The main columns at Karnak which once supported the roof were almost seventy feet high (twelve times as high as a man standing up) and twelve feet wide (twice as thick as a man's length when he is lying down). These columns were made to look either like a single lotus flower or a bouquet of lotus flowers. Lotus flowers were water lilies that grew in the Nile. Unfortunately, many of these Egyptian ruins are being flooded as dams are built on the Nile River.

---

right: The main columns at Karnak

Trans World Airlines, Inc.

Egyptian State Tourist Administration. Photo by C. Zachary.

Egyptian State Tourist Administration. Photo by C. Zachary.

UAR Information Center. Embassy of the United Arab Republic.

opposite left: Statues of Rameses II at Karnak

opposite right: A Karnak Column

left: Lion Statues at Karnak

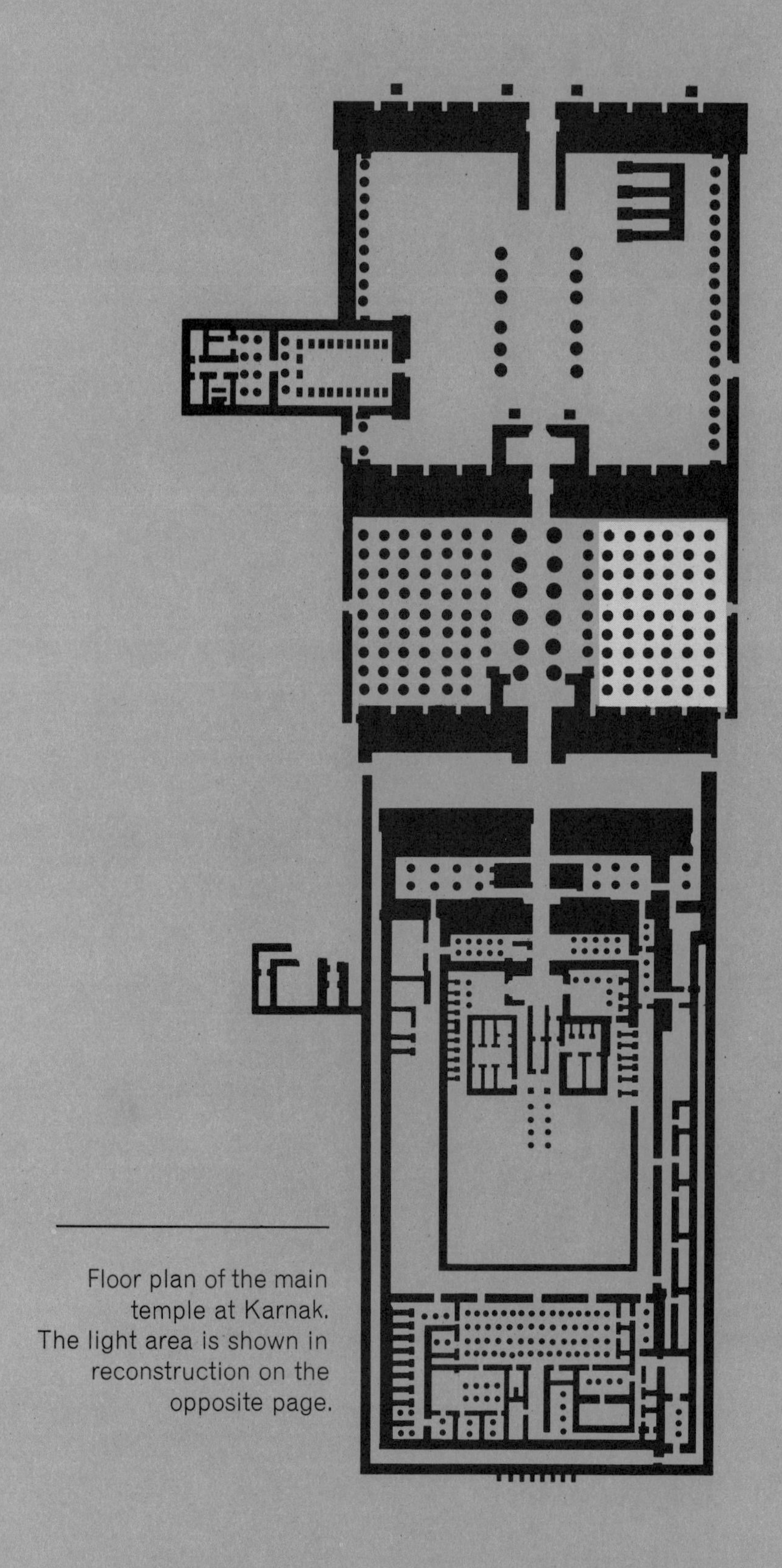

Floor plan of the main temple at Karnak. The light area is shown in reconstruction on the opposite page.

Reconstruction of a section of the main hall of columns at Karnak (Hypostyle Hall)

There are other Egyptian temples, but though all of them are smaller, all were built in somewhat the same way. First there was an avenue of sphinxes leading to the temple, and then there were two *obelisks*. An obelisk is a tall, upright stone pointed at the top. It was supposed to represent a ray of the sun.

After the obelisks came the gateway to the temple. This was made with two huge towers called *pylons*, one at each side of the door. The pylon walls slant inward, and if they went higher they would meet like a pyramid. It is thought that the old astrologers—men who told fortunes from the stars—used to go up on top of these pylons to "read the stars." The front of these pylons had figures cut into the rock face.

Behind the gateway was a walled courtyard, and behind that was a hall of columns called a *hypostyle hall*, and behind that the holy place where the statue of the god was kept.

Many of the obelisks in Egypt have been taken to other countries. Some of them have been given away, some have been bought, some have been stolen. There is one in Central Park, New York, and there is another in London, on the bank of the river Thames. These two obelisks are called *Cleopatra's Needles*, though they were made long before the queen of Egypt named Cleopatra lived; they looked more like giant pencils than needles. One is in Paris in the center of a beautiful square. There are many in Rome.

opposite, top left: Obelisk of Theodosius brought to Istanbul, Turkey, from Heliopolis, Egypt

---

opposite, top right: Pylon of a temple in Egypt

---

opposite bottom: Obelisk in St. Peter's Square, Rome

Office of the Turkish Press Counselor, Washington, D.C.

Historical Pictures Service, Chicago

Photograph by Ente Provinciale per il Turismo—Rome

Builders of the Two River Country

In the Bible, *Chaldeans* means the wise men and priests of what we will call the Two River Country. They were men of Chaldea, which was one of the countries in the Two River Country along with Assyria and Babylonia. Assyria was a little farther north than Babylonia and Chaldea, but all three countries were very much alike and sometimes all three were under one king. This area today is called Iraq.

The Two River Country was watered by a network of canals between the Two Rivers, the Tigris and the Euphrates, and so was very fertile. The finest crops in all the world grew there and many large cities were built on the plains. Today these plains are dry and desert-like, for the canals have not been taken care of and without water the crops fail to grow. On the plains one can now see big mounds or low hills where once the palaces and cities stood. These are all that is left of the handsome buildings of this ancient land. They crumbled into dust because they were made of *mud.* Imagine a king's palace made of mud—mud baked in the sun like a mud pie! But these Two River people covered their mud walls with glazed tiles and slabs of stone. The tiles were brightly colored like today's bathroom tiles and the slabs of stone were carved in low relief so that even a mud palace became a handsome building.

But with only mud bricks the Two River builders were handicapped. They could not make mud-brick houses more than one story high. The houses would have tumbled down had they been higher. The walls were not strong enough to hold a second story. Since a one-story house would not look very palace-like, when these people built a palace they first made a hill with a flat top or platform of dried mud and placed the palace on that. The palace then seemed much higher.

The sides of the platform were very steep—almost straight up and down. So to reach the top of the platform a slanting roadway called a ramp was built against its side.

Because mud walls were so crumbly, the builders had to make their palace walls very, very thick. Some were as much as twenty feet thick. The sun was very hot in that part of the world and these thick walls helped to keep out the heat. To keep out the heat even more, the Two River people made their palaces without windows, so the rooms were lighted only by lamps.

We usually think of palace rooms as large and spacious, but the rooms in the Two Rivers mud palaces were very small. They had to be because of the lack of stone and of wooden beams long enough to stretch across a wide space. In a palace, however, the builders made up for the smallness of the rooms by having a great number of them.

The temples that the priests built were made of mud bricks, too, but the one single platform for a foundation was not enough, so they built several, one on top of another. This gave the effect of a terraced pyramid, for each platform was set back from the one below it. Architects today sometimes plan tall buildings—skyscrapers—in this ancient way, with the stories stepped back.

Historical Pictures Service, Chicago

Restoration of the Palace of Ninevah

The Bible story of the flood tells how the Babylonians built a tower called the Tower of Babel so that in case of another flood the people could climb to the top and escape drowning. The Tower of Babel was not built straight up and down. It was a stepped pyramid such as I have described. It was like a set of blocks of different sizes piled one on top of another, each one a little smaller than the one below. Each was reached from the other by a ramp. On the topmost and smallest platform was placed the temple or shrine for the idol.

The Tower of Babel was supposed to have had seven giant steps or terraces. Seven was thought to be a magic number. Each step was in honor of one of the heavenly bodies. The topmost terrace, in honor of the sun, was covered with gold. The next, in honor of the moon, was covered with silver. Those below, in honor of each of five planets, were painted in different colors.

The Chaldeans were the first to make a study of the stars and their movements in the sky, and they gave many of the stars names that we still use. We call such people astronomers. The Chaldean astronomers used the temple on top of these terraced pyramids or towers for an observatory—that is, a place from which to observe the heavenly bodies. That is why the Chaldeans came to be known as the wise men of the Two River Country.

There is an old saying that "necessity is the mother of invention." That means if you haven't what you need, you will invent something to supply your need. It was necessity that made the Assyrians invent one of the most important building ideas that we use today. This was called the *principle of the arch.*

The Assyrians had no stones long enough to stretch from one side to the other of a large room to form the ceiling, so they had to invent a way of covering a room or a doorway with small pieces of stone or bricks. You might call an open doorway an arch, but one piece of stone or wood laid across an opening does not make an arch. An arch must be made of several pieces.

Arrangement of bricks or stones used to form an arch

It is nearly impossible to cement bricks or small stones together strongly enough to make them into one piece that will stretch from wall to wall and not fall. But if you arrange wedge-shaped stones in a curve or half circle, they will not fall. This is an arch.

By this simple arrangement, the stones are made to stay in place, not because they are stuck together, for they will stay in place whether they are cemented or not, but because each stone, pressing downward, trying to fall through, presses against the stones at each side. They are all so tightly jammed together that none can squeeze through and fall. The heavier the weight on top of the arch, the more firmly are the wedge-shaped stones held in place, provided there is no way for them to push over the side wall and widen the space. To prevent the stones of an arch from slipping, the side walls of arches were made very heavy and thick.

Italian State Tourist Office-Enit. Foto Enit-Roma.

Barrel vault room

Italian State Tourist Office-Enit. Foto Enit-Roma.

Construction of a dome

Not only doorways but whole rooms could be covered in this same way. When a room was covered, the arch became what was called a barrel vault, for the ceiling of such a vaulted room was like half a barrel. If the room itself had circular walls, the ceiling became a bowl turned upside down. We call the bowl a dome, but the principle was the same—the principle of the arch.

While an arch or vault or dome was being built, it was necessary to have something to build the stones upon, for until the last stone was in place, the arch would not hold. Usually a temporary framework of wood, shaped like a half circle, called *centering*, was therefore placed across from one wall to the other. On top of this the arch was built, starting at each side and working toward the top. When the last stone at the top, which was called the keystone, was put in place, then, and not until then, could the centering be knocked down and the arch would stand alone. In Assyria, however, there was so little wood for making centering that few arches or vaults were made. It was not until a thousand years or so later that arches were used frequently.

In Egypt, the pyramids are still standing because they were made of stone and built in the most lasting shape there is. They cannot topple over or fall down. In the Two River Country not a single palace or temple is still standing. The bricks of which they were built have crumbled into dust again, so all that is now left are the mounds of earth overgown with weeds.

It seems impossible to believe that our great cities of today may ever become just heaps of dirt, grown over with weeds like the old Assyrian and Babylonian cities, or that the millions of people now living in the houses and thronging the streets should ever disappear. Yet the people who lived in Assyria probably thought the same thing.

upper left: Interior view of the dome of St. Peter's, Rome

lower left: Exterior view of the dome of St. Peter's, Rome

The Perfect Parthenon

If you make a mistake in arithmetic or composition, you can correct it or tear it up and do it over. If a picture or a statue is ugly, it can be put out of sight, hidden, or destroyed. But if a building is ugly, there it stands for everyone to see. Its ugliness or its mistakes cannot be covered up until it falls down or is torn down. An architect once committed suicide just as the great temple he had planned was finished. He left a note saying that he had made five mistakes in the building and since they could not be corrected and could not be covered up, there they were for everyone to see forever. He could not stand the disgrace.

Most buildings that are erected have many mistakes, many things that are ugly about them, though few people may notice anything wrong.

But there was one building that was erected over two thousand years ago that has no mistakes. It is one of the few perfect buildings in the world. It was built for a woman, in honor of a Greek goddess, the goddess of wisdom, whose name was Athene Parthenos. The building was called after her last name, the Parthenon. It is on a high hill in the city of Athens, in Greece, and though it has been partly destroyed, people go to Athens from all over the world to see what a perfect building looks like.

Mt. Acropolis, Athens, Greece. The Parthenon is the many-columned building at the top of opposite page.

Trans World Airlines, Inc.

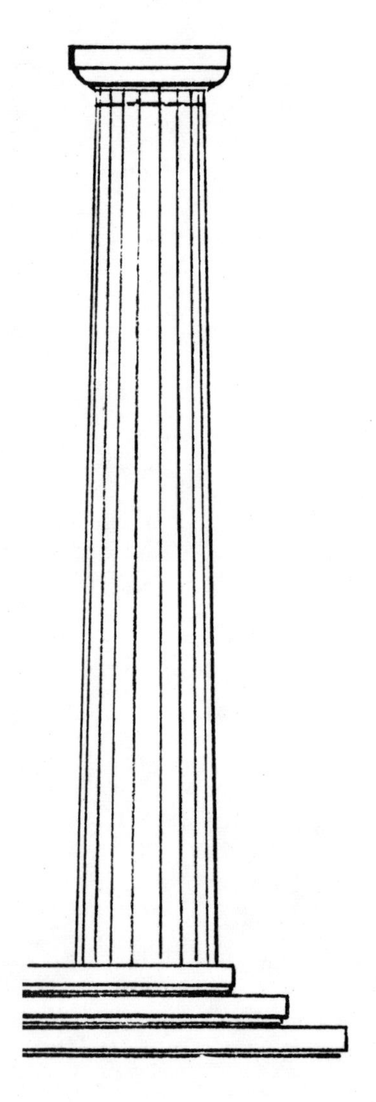

The Egyptian temples had flat roofs because there was little or no rain in Egypt, so a sloping roof to shed the rain was not necessary. The Greek temples had to have slanting roofs, for Greece had rain. So the Parthenon had a sloping roof.

The Egyptians built their temples with the columns on the inside. The Greeks turned the Egyptian temple inside out and put the columns on the outside. The Greek temple was not to hold people, but only the statue of the goddess. People didn't go inside to worship as they do in churches today. They stood on the outside. The columns the Greeks used were not like those the Egyptians used. They were simpler, but much more beautiful.

Greek temples had three kinds of columns. The kind used in the Parthenon was the *Doric* column, the "man's style" column. It is called Doric after a very old Greek tribe. Not only the column but the style of building that always went with this particular column was strong, simple, plain. That's why it is called the man's style. There were many Doric buildings in Greece, but the Parthenon was the most beautiful of all.

A Doric building is built on a terraced or stepped platform and is not made of mud bricks plated with alabaster or tile as the Two River people built their

---

left: A Doric Column

temples, but of solid stone, usually marble. There was no cheating in Greek building. It was what it seemed to be.

Styles in ladies' hats and clothes change often, as you know, but the Doric style of building lasted over two thousand years. I'll try to describe it so you can tell it when you see it.

The Doric column has no base, but rests directly on the platform. It tapers slightly as a tree trunk does. Its sides are not perfectly straight. They may look so, but as a matter of fact, they bulge slightly. This bulge is called *entasis*. A column was given entasis because one that had straight sides, one without entasis, looked as if it were *thinner* in the middle.

Some architects of today, noticing this slight bulge in the Doric column, have thought they would improve on it by making the bulge greater. Some people, when the doctor says take one pill, take two, reasoning that if one pill is good for you, two will be better. But the Greek entasis was just exactly enough; more entasis makes a column look fat and ugly like a man who is fat around the middle.

The sides of the Doric column were then *fluted*—cut with grooves so as to make slender, lengthwise shadows from top to bottom of the column and thus take away from the plainness that a perfectly smooth column would have. Most columns today have no fluting. You can imagine how difficult it is to cut such channels in marble without making a single slip. One single slip would ruin the column and it couldn't be repaired.

The top of the column is called the *capital* because capital means head. The capital was made of a piece shaped like a saucer, above which was a thin square block. You'll have to look at the picture to understand the rest.

There may be some Doric building where you live. It may be a bank or a library, a courthouse or some other building. Examine it and see if it has all these things that a perfect Doric building has, and only these things.

Are the columns of stone or only of wood?

Are they fluted or only plain?

Has it the proper capital and other parts as in the true Doric style?

Men have tried ever since the time the Parthenon was built to improve on the Doric temple, but it seems impossible to do so. Every change that is made from the original is less beautiful.

It takes a good eye to tell when a building's proportions are right or wrong. The Greeks had what we call "a good eye" for a building's looks. Some people can't tell when a picture is hanging straight on the wall. They may even measure the distance and declare it straight, but a person with a "good eye" can detect what the ruler may not show—that it is tipped the smallest bit, just a hair's breadth perhaps.

There are two important tools that a builder today uses—a plumb bob and a level. A plumb bob tells whether a wall or a column or anything else supposed to be straight up and down *is* really straight up and down or vertical, as it is called. A level, which has a little bubble in a glass on its edge, tells whether a floor or a sill or anything else supposed to be level *is* really level or horizontal, as it is called. You can't fool a plumb bob or a level.

But the Greeks said you couldn't believe the plumb bob or the level, for columns that are really vertical seem to lean out and floors that are really horizontal seem to sag in the middle. That's because our eyes make them seem so. Since we see buildings with our eyes, the Greek builders of the Parthenon built it as they wanted the eyes to see it, and so, though all lines may *seem* to be vertical, horizontal, level, or straight, there is really not a vertical line or a horizontal line or a perfectly straight line in the Parthenon. That's one of the things that makes the Parthenon so extraordinary!

The columns were not made of single blocks of stone, but of drum-shaped pieces that were cut with such exactitude that they fitted perfectly and no crack showed. It is even said that the pieces have grown together like a broken bone that is well set!

Ionic Masterpiece, the Erechtheum

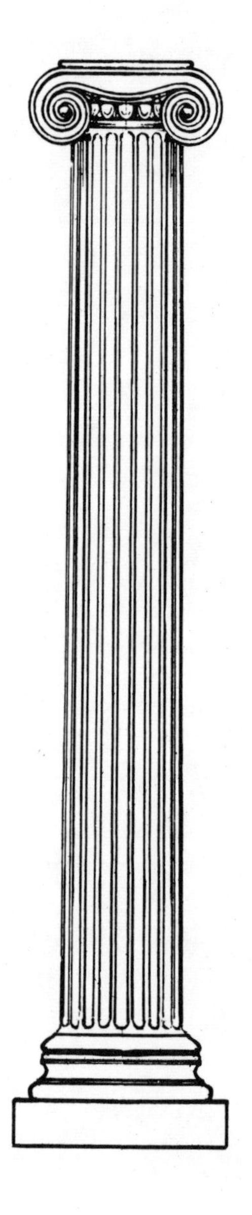

It may seem rather farfetched to say a building is like a woman, but the ancient Greeks had farfetched imaginations. They imagined, for instance, that a vain boy had been turned into the flower we call the narcissus; that a girl who dared to love the beautiful sun god was turned into the sunflower; and that a nymph had been turned into a laurel tree. So it was not such a great stretch of the imagination, after all, for them to say that a woman had been turned into a certain kind of column or that a certain kind of marble column was like a woman.

An architect named Vitruvius, who lived a hundred years before Christ, said that the two curls on the head of this column were the locks of the woman's hair; that the grooves or flutings in the body of the column were the folds of her gown; and that the base was her bare feet. They called this kind of column *Ionic* because it was first made in Ionia, a colony of Greece across the sea in Asia Minor.

The best Ionic building was in Athens on the Acropolis, near the Doric temple, the Parthenon. It was called the Erechtheum because it was built in honor of Erechtheus, who was supposed to have been a king of Athens in days long past.

left: An Ionic Column

opposite: The capital of an Ionic column at the Acropolis, Athens, Greece.

The Parthenon was a man's style building built in honor of a woman. The Erechtheum was a woman's style building built in honor of a man. Ionic columns were on three sides of the Erechtheum, but on the fourth end of the same building there are six statues of real women in place of columns. They hold the roof on their heads. It is called the Porch of the Maidens. So in the same temple there are not only the woman's style columns, but the actual women's figures. The women's figures are called *Caryatids*. The story is that they represented captives from Carya condemned to stand in this position, holding the roof on their heads, forever. One of the Caryatids was taken to England and in its place was put a copy made of terra cotta.

---

opposite: The Erechtheum, Acropolis, Athens, Greece

National Tourist Organization of Greece

Historical Pictures Service, Chicago

Porch of the Maidens, The Erechtheum, Athens

The largest and most famous Ionic temple in the world was not in Greece itself. It was in Ionia, at Ephesus. It was built to Diana, the goddess of the moon, and was so magnificent that it was called one of the Seven Wonders of the World. A Bible story tells about Saint Paul nearly starting a riot there by preaching against Diana, whom the Christians called a heathen goddess. The mob wouldn't listen to him. To drown out what Saint Paul was trying to say against their goddess, they cried aloud for two hours: "Great is Diana of the Ephesians! Great is Diana of the Ephesians!" The temple has disappeared (all but the floor), but the sayings of Saint Paul, which the Ephesians tried to drown out, still last.

Another one of the Seven Wonders of the World was another Ionic building at a place called Halicarnassus. It was not a temple, however, but a tomb built for King Mausolus by his widow. Though this tomb is no more, we still call any very large tomb a mausoleum, after the tomb of Mausolus.

You don't have to go to Greece to see Ionic columns. There are probably many Ionic buildings where you live, but see if they are the true Ionic, or what we call *hybrid*. That means a mixture, as a dog that is part fox terrier and part bull terrier is a mixture, a mongrel, a hybrid.

Architects used the Ionic style more often than they did the Doric, so if you should try to count the number of Ionic and Doric columns you can find in the place where you live, you would probably count several times as many Ionic as Doric.

---

opposite: Porch of the Maidens, The Erechtheum, Athens

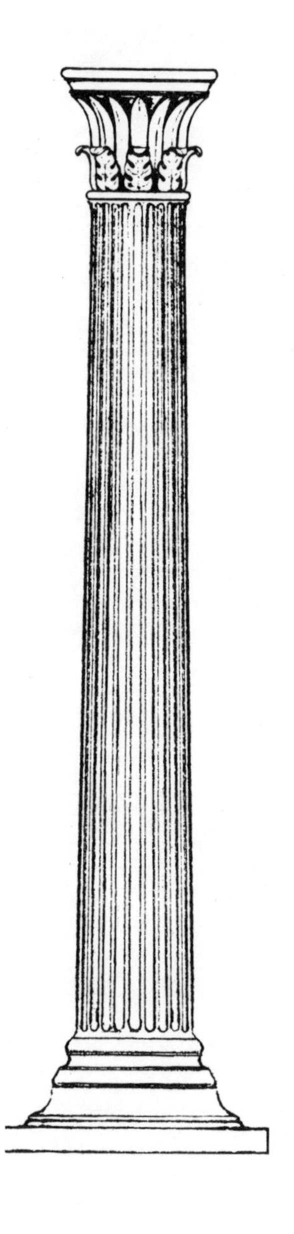

Roman Builders

People get tired of seeing the same styles in dresses and hats and try to start something new. Many women today go to Paris for their styles. In the same way, architects used to go to Greece for their styles in buildings. Some architects have tried to start new styles in columns just to have something new and different, but the columns they have invented have all been less beautiful than the two Greek columns I have described.

The Greeks started a new style of column called the *Corinthian,* but they didn't like it very much themselves and hardly used it at all. The old architect Vitruvius, who told us the story of the Ionic column, tells us another legend to explain the Corinthian capital.

Vitruvius said that a basket of toys with a tile over the top was placed on the grave of a little girl in Corinth, as was the custom in those days. By chance, the basket had been placed directly over a thistle plant and the leaves of the thistle grew up around the basket. An architect, seeing

left: A Corinthian Column

this basket with the leaves curling around it, thought it would make a good design for a capital of a column, so he copied it in marble and put it on an Ionic column in place of the Ionic capital. In this way the Corinthian column was invented.

So the Corinthian column is just an Ionic column with a different capital. The Greek thistle is called the *acanthus*, so the leaves that curl upward and outward on each side of the Corinthian capital are acanthus leaves. Just underneath the tile, which is called the *abacus*, are four corner scrolls or curls. They are like curl shavings the carpenter makes with his plane, but not like those of the Ionic capital, which are like rolls of music. The Ionic curls faced front and back, but the Corithian curls faced cornerwise.

Many people think the Corinthian capital is more beautiful than either the Doric or the Ionic, but others think it is too fancy and not natural to have stone beams resting on leaves.

The Greeks finished all their great buildings about three hundred years before Christ was born, and all their great architects seem to have died, for no great ones lived after that time.

You may know that Greece is nearly an island, called a peninsula, in the Mediterranean Sea. Next door to Greece is another near-island, or peninsula, called Italy. The capital of Italy was Rome, and after Greece had lost her power Rome became the capital—that is, the head—of most of the world.

The Greeks were great architects, but the Romans were great builders. There is a difference. The Romans built many fine buildings, but their taste wasn't as good as that of the Greeks. The Romans liked the Corinthian column better than either the Doric or the Ionic. The Romans also made another column *composed* of both the Ionic and Corinthian capitals. This column is called *Composite.* It had the large curls, or *volutes,* of the Ionic and the acanthus leaves of the Corinthian. Often it is hard to tell whether a column is Corinthian or Composite. In the Composite column, the Ionic top is larger than in the Corinthian. The Romans also changed the Doric column—gave it a base and left out the flutings and the saucer-shaped part of the capital. This kind of Roman column was called *Etruscan Doric* or *Tuscan.*

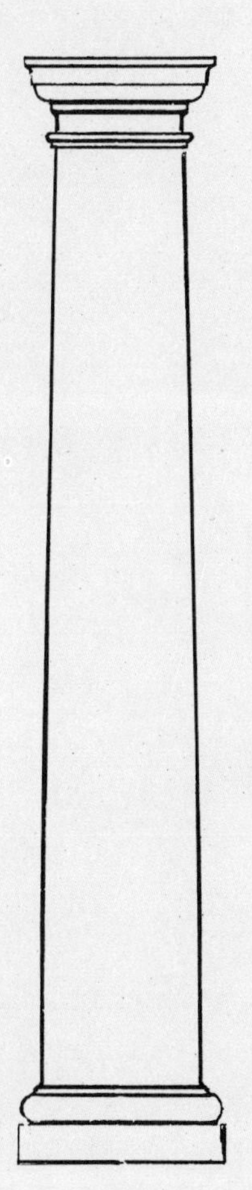

opposite left: The capital of a Corinthian column

opposite right: The capital of a Composite column

right: An Etruscan Doric column

The Romans made other changes in their styles of building—changes for the worse. In order to make columns seem higher than they were, they frequently put a boxlike base or pedestal beneath each column. They also placed split columns, or half columns, against walls. Such half columns built against the wall are called *engaged*. Other columns they flattened out against the wall so that they appeared square. A column so flattened out is called a *pilaster*.

The greatest thing the Romans did for building was to use the arch. As you know, the Assyrians invented the arch but used it very little because they had very little stone with which to build arches. But they never rested their arches on columns. The Greeks and other architects before them placed a single stone across from column to column. This, you remember, is called the post and lintel. But a single slab of stone could not reach very far, so the spaces between columns were never very great and never could be very great. The Romans were the first to make arches from column to column.

The Romans also made barrel vaults and domes which, you remember, were arched ceilings built on the same principle as the arch. By using the dome and the vault, they were able to roof over much larger spaces than could have been roofed over with single slabs of stone or with wooden roofs. Furthermore, a vaulted or domed roof of stone was fireproof, whereas a wooden roof, of course, was not.

Another great thing the Romans did for building was to use cement and concrete. The Romans used cement between the stones of their arches as a type of glue. They used concrete, which is a mixture of cement with water and sand and pebbles, for their domes and vaults. Concrete turns into stone when it dries. Now, an arch or a dome or a vault, if properly put together, needs no cement, for the stones push against one another so tightly they can't slip through and down. But, as I have told you, an arch does need heavy walls at the side so that the stone in the arch will not push over the walls, for the weight of each stone pushes and shoves sideways.

The Romans found a way out of this difficulty. They held together the stones of their vaults and domes with cement or concrete so that the vault or dome became a single solid stone. Such a concrete dome pushes downward but doesn't push sideways, so that heavy side walls are not really necessary.

You can rest a trunk or a piano or an automobile on blocks or bricks and the trunk or piano will not fall. But if the blocks or bricks are pushed sideways the least bit, the load they carry will fall. Have you ever stood up a row of blocks or bricks and tried to walk across them? Try it. If you press straight down as you step on them, they will not fall, but if you shove them sideways the least little bit, over they go! Well, it's the same with a load on a column or a wall. As I have explained, if the load presses straight down, a small column or small wall will hold the load perfectly well; but the separate stones in an arch do not push straight down. They push sideways, so the wall must be made very heavy to keep from being pushed over by an arch. However, when there is a *row* of arches on columns, each arch pushes against the next arch and the next arch pushes back so that there is no side push on the columns.

Arches push and shove. You may not see it, but they do. Try pushing against someone who pushes against you. You can lean together like the sides of a letter A, but if one suddenly stops pushing or jumps aside, down the other goes. That's the way one arch pushes against another. Knock away one arch and down the other goes.

---

opposite: Amphitheater, Arles. Interior view looking north toward the main entrance.

Historical Pictures Service, Chicago

Roman Buildings

Some people wear imitation pearls, imitation diamonds, imitation jewelry, just for show. Some people build houses of concrete blocks to imitate stone, paint wooden columns to imitate marble, cover plaster walls with paper to imitate tile or brick. Such imitations that pretend to be something they are not, are a kind of cheating, a fake. The Greeks never faked in this way. The Romans often did so. They built buildings of concrete or brick and covered the outside with thin pieces of marble.

For a few hundred years before and after Christ was born, the Romans built and built, many buildings, great buildings, and more buildings of more kinds than had ever been built before. They built them not only in Rome and in Italy, but in other countries the Romans controlled.

Though the Romans built many great buildings, none of them quite equaled those the Greeks built. The reason was that the Romans were not artists but engineers. The Greeks were very religious and built temples; the Romans were great governors and worshiped everything that concerned governing. The Romans used instruments to design their buildings, whereas the Greeks used their eyes.

In a Roman building, every line that was supposed to be vertical *was* vertical. Every line that was supposed to be horizontal *was* horizontal. Every line that was supposed to be straight *was* straight. It was as if they had drawn a picture with a ruler and square and compass instead of freehand.

In the same way, a Roman building looks mechanical. We like them in the same way we like an engine. They are strong and powerful, but somehow seem to lack the beauty of a handmade picture.

How many kinds of buildings do you think there are in the place where you live? Try to count them. Houses, of course, but how many others—stores, libraries, churches, temples, banks, courthouses, and so on.

The Greeks had only a few, but the Romans built many kinds—not only tombs and temples, houses and palaces, but also arches and aqueducts, bridges and baths, courthouses and halls, theaters and amphitheaters.

Some were fake, but not all, and some were magnificent and imposing. Most of the Roman buildings are now in ruins, but one building, a temple built to all the gods, is still standing and in use today. It is called the Pantheon, which means "All the Gods." It has a porch in front with Corinthian columns; behind the porch is a circular building with a huge dome made like a bowl turned upside down, of concrete. The circular walls that support the dome are twenty feet thick and the only window is a large circular opening in the top of the dome. There is no glass in the opening, but it is so high above the floor that even a heavy rain barely wets the floor beneath.

Italian State Tourist Office-Enit. Foto Enit-Roma.

French Cultural Services

above: La Maison Carrée (The Square House)

opposite: Roman Pantheon

The Square House is one of the finest of these Roman buildings, with engaged Corinthian columns as well as with whole columns. It is not in Rome, however. It is in what is now France. It was built by Romans when France was a part of the Roman Empire. In France they call it the Maison Carrée, which means Square House.

The theaters in which Roman actors gave plays had no roofs. The seats were of stone and were arranged in a half circle that sloped upward as in theaters today. In France, at a town called Orange, is a Roman theater in which plays are still given.

Nero, one of the rulers of Rome, built himself an enormous palace surrounded by parks and lakes. It was called the Golden House. Later rulers destroyed it. He built a colossal statue of himself which some writers say was 120 feet high. Only its base still exists.

Near where the colossal statue of Nero was, a huge amphitheater was built later. It was called the Colosseum. An amphitheater was something like a football stadium, but instead of games, there were fights held between men and men, or between men and wild animals. The Colosseum had stone seats arranged in an oval shape. The outside walls were four stories high; the lower three stories were rows of arches. Between the arches on the first or ground floor there were engaged Doric columns. Between the arches of the second story were engaged Ionic columns. Between those of the third floor were engaged Corinthian, and on the fourth-story wall were Composite pilasters.

French Cultural Services

---

opposite: The Roman Theater at Orange

Trans World Airlines, Inc.

Colosseum,
Rome

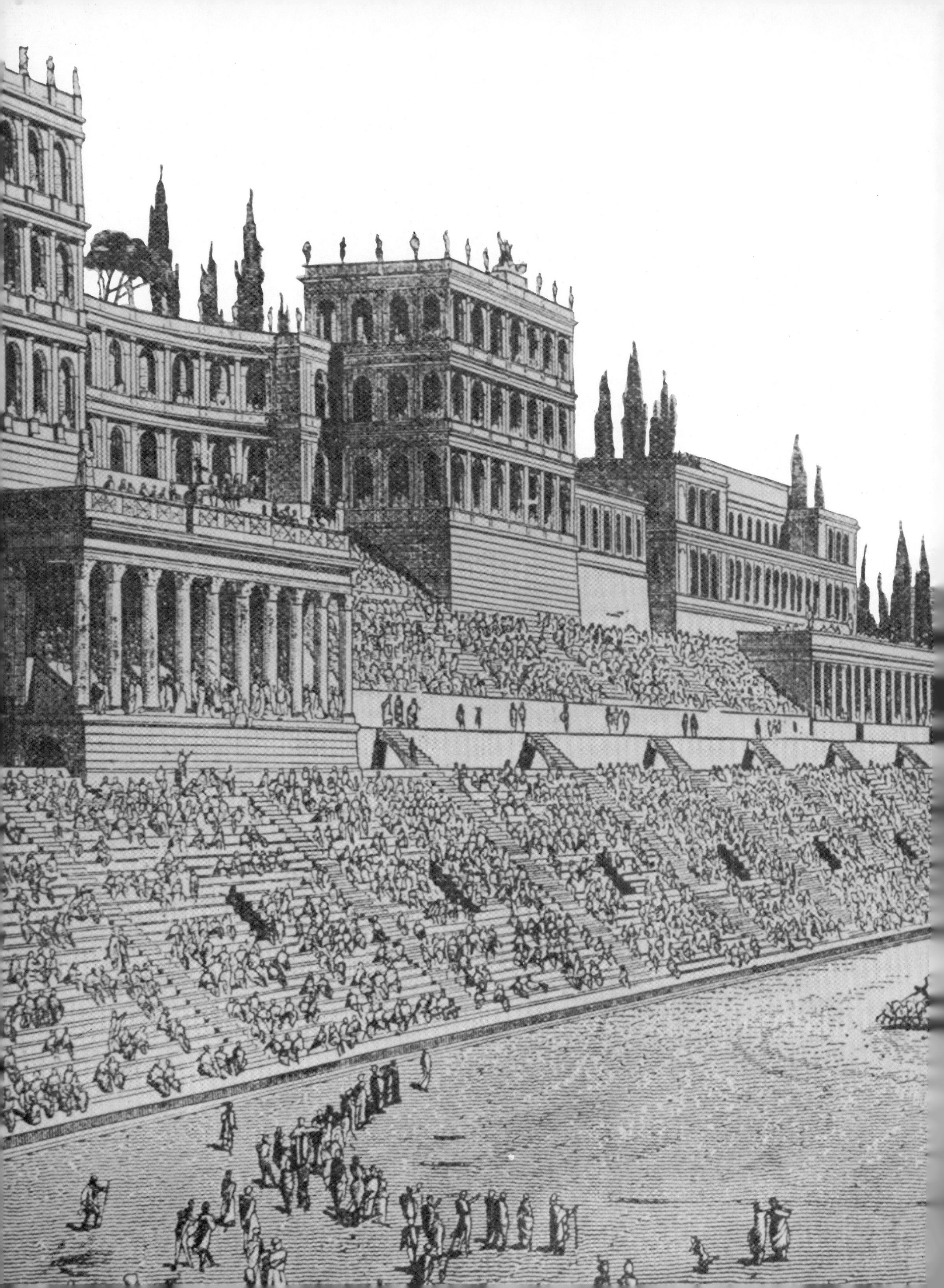

The Colosseum is now a ruin, but a great part of it is still standing. The amphitheater held as many people as a large stadium does today, but there was a still larger one called the Circus Maximus which held many more people than the largest stadium today holds. Circus in this case doesn't mean a circus; it means a ring, and Circus Maximus meant the "largest ring." Most of the huge Circus Maximus has completely disappeared but some of its foundations still remain.

The race course in the Circus Maximus, Rome

Historical Pictures Service, Chicago

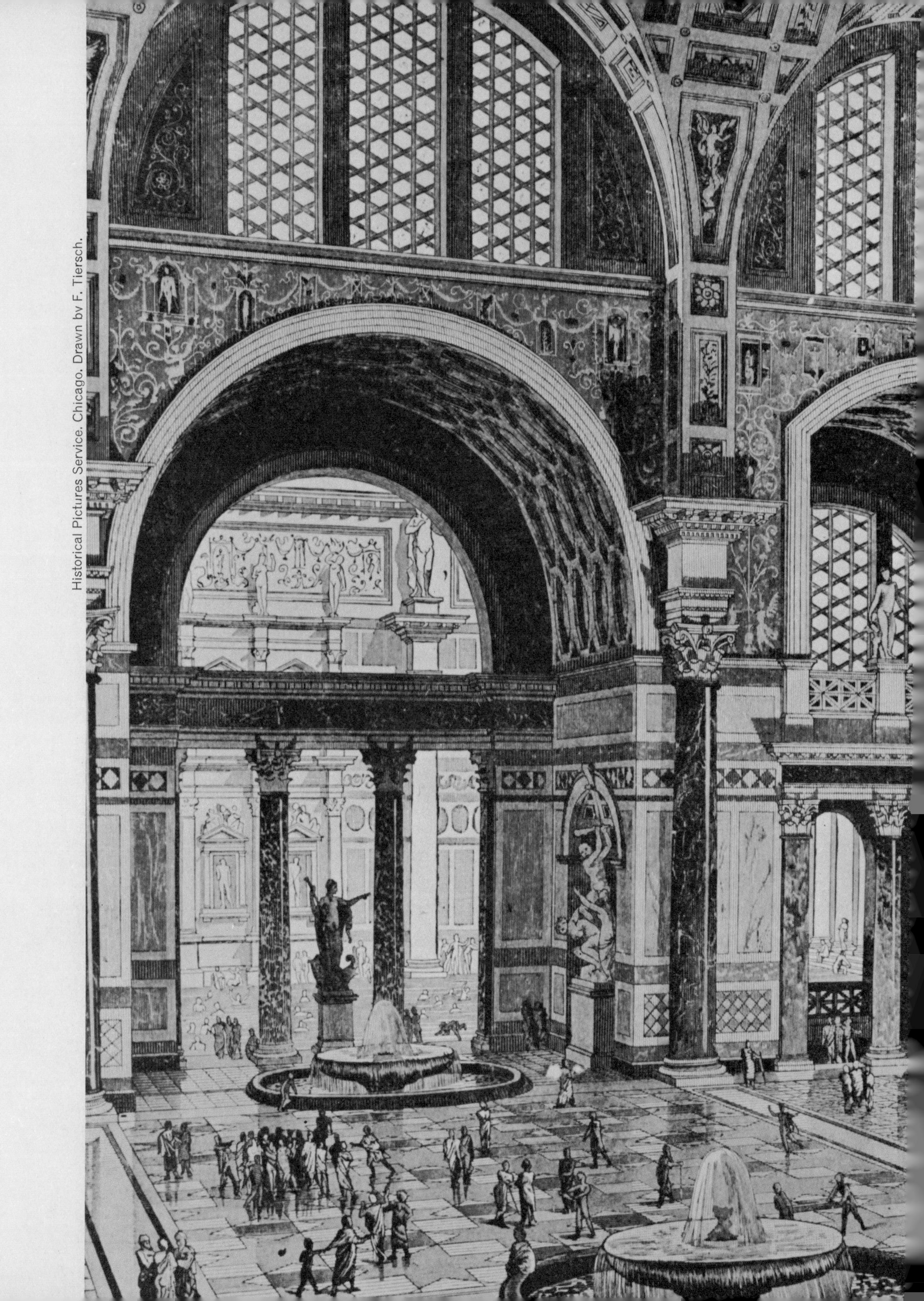

Historical Pictures Service, Chicago. Drawn by F. Tiersch.

Photograph by Ente Provinciale per il Turismo—Rome

above: Arch of Titus, Rome

---

opposite: The baths of Caracalla, Rome

The Romans built public bathhouses, for the common people had no baths at all in their homes. These baths were huge buildings with arched or vaulted rooms in which a thousand or more people could bathe at one time. There were not only hot and cold and warm baths, but gymnasiums, game rooms, lounging rooms, and so on. They were public places for amusement and recreation.

The Romans built large arches, separate from buildings, just for their rulers who had won great battles to march through with their soldiers. Such arches were called Triumphal Arches. One, called the Arch of Titus, was built to celebrate his conquest and destruction of the city of Jerusalem. The Arch of Titus has one large single arch.

Another arch, the Arch of Constantine, was built in honor of that ruler who was the first emperor of Rome to become a Christian. The Arch of Constantine has one large arch and two smaller arches, one at each side.

Italian State Tourist Office-Enit. Foto Enit-Roma.

Arch of Constantine, Rome

Historical Pictures Service, Chicago

The bridges the Romans built were among the strongest and most substantial structures they made. Some of these bridges were built not for people to walk across, but for water to run through. On the top of such a bridge was a trough through which water flowed from its source to the city. It was like a river held up by a bridge. Such a bridge of arches carrying water was called an *aqueduct*, which means water pipe or water carrier. These days water is usually brought to a city from a river or lake or reservoir, through large pipes which may run underground and uphill and downhill. But the Romans built aqueducts instead of pipes to carry water to a city, and these aqueducts—some of them over fifty miles long—sloped just enough so that the water was always running downhill.

Roman Aqueduct at Nimes

Italian State Tourist Office-Enit. Foto Enit-Roma.

The Romans made one other kind of building from which later Christian churches were copied. These buildings were courthouses or public halls and were called *basilicas*. Basilicas were long buildings with rows of columns on the inside which held up the roof. There were a center aisle and two side aisles; the roof over the center aisle was higher than the roof over the side aisles, as is the case in most churches today.

opposite: Roman Basilica of San Giovanni in Laterano

Moldings and Borders

Men wear ties and collars. Ladies wear ornaments and trimmings. Buildings have trimmings, too, to keep them from looking too plain and unfinished. These trimmings on buildings are called *moldings* and *borders.* The Greek and Roman builders used moldings and borders of certain shapes and designs, and builders today use many of the same moldings and borders.

Perhaps you have never examined closely the panels of a door, the edges of a doorway or window, or other trimmings around the outside of a building, but if you should notice them, you may be surprised to see that many of them are not just flat strips. They have different shapes.

There is a molding that is square as seen from the edge, and very simple. It is called a *fillet,* which means a ribbon or band. In ancient times women—and men, too—wore a

fillet around their heads to keep their hair in place and as an ornament. Today, buildings often have fillets as ornaments. A fillet, as seen from the edge, looks like our illustration.

When a fillet is sunken in, like a square groove, it is called a *sunken fillet.*

A molding that is half round as seen from the edge is called a *torus* by architects, but to carpenters it is a "half-round."

The torus, or half-round, sunk in to form a round hollow or groove is called a *cavetto,* which means a little cave. Carpenters call it a groove.

A molding that looks like the curve of an egg when seen from the edge is called by architects an *ovolo,* which means egg-shaped; carpenters just say "egg molding."

A molding that is hollowed out with the same egg-shaped curve is called a *scotia.*

A molding with a curve like an S with the hollow at the bottom, is called an *ogee.*

Another molding with an S curve has the hollow at the top. It is called a *cyma,* which means a wave.

Do you think you can recognize these moldings when you see them and remember their names? They are in pairs—four pairs. One is raised and one is hollow; one fits into the other:

fillet—sunken fillet
torus—cavetto
ovolo—scotia
ogee—cyma

Usually, instead of just one molding, two or more of these moldings are used, one alongside another. Several beautiful moldings are made by such combinations.

In most of the combinations, the square fillet is used between the curved moldings. This arrangement of square and curve makes the curved moldings stand out more sharply.

See how many of these moldings you can find.

There are also several kinds of borders. The simplest is the zigzag, which is also called the *chevron* because it is like the chevron that a soldier wears on his sleeve.

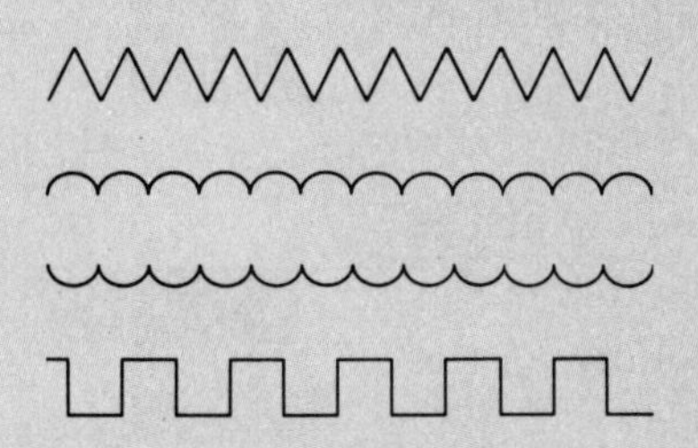

The next simplest is the *scallop*. It is called that because it is like the edge of the scallop shell. It may be used rightside up or upside down.

The *embattled* border is sometimes called the Wall of Troy, because Troy had a wall around it, with spaces through which the soldiers could shoot their arrows, and pieces of wall behind which they could jump.

The *meander* is named after the Meander River in Asia Minor; it flowed in this very crooked way. If you walk in a line that makes a design like this, we say you are meandering.

The *fret* or *key* looks something like a row of keys.

The *dentil* is supposed to look like a row of teeth. "Dentil" means teeth. It looks something like a row of piano keys, too.

The *wave* looks something like an S lying down with a curl or scroll in one end. You can see why it is called this if you have ever seen waves breaking on the shore.

The *running scroll* looks like one wave up and one down. This is one of the prettiest borders.

Another border is the *astragal.* Astragals were really little bones, but the astragal border looks something like a string of long beads with two round beads between them.

Other borders are the *chain,* the *cable* or *rope,* and the *egg and dart.* The egg was supposed to represent birth; the dart, death—birth and death, birth and death. Every man is born and dies. His son is born and dies. Generation after generation is born and dies, forever and ever. The astragal was always used below the egg and dart border.

The *anthemion*—leaves arranged in a heart shape—was often used in an alternating pattern with the *Greek lily.*

These are called classic borders because the Greeks and Romans used them, and anything Greek and Roman we call classic.

Early Christian Architecture

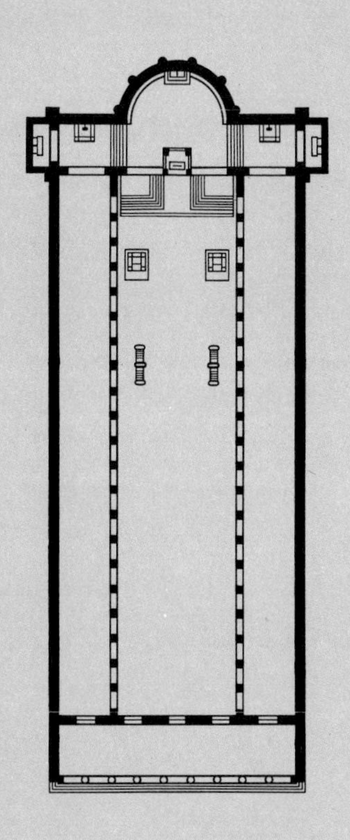

Plan of a Basilica

In architecture, *early Christian* means early in the history of Christians. Some of our finest buildings today are Christian churches, but long ago the only Christian churches were holes in the ground called *catacombs.* They were tunnels that were dug underground in Rome because the Christians were persecuted—punished for being Christians—and had to live in hiding. They hid in the dark secret passages of the catacombs. In the catacombs were rooms where Christians could worship; there were rooms there, too, where Christians could bury their dead safely.

It was like living in a coal mine, only worse, because when a Christian was caught by the Roman soldiers, he was usually given to the lions or burned alive or chopped to pieces.

The Christians who lived in the catacombs must have been very happy when the Roman emperor himself became a Christian. This first Christian emperor was named Constantine. When Constantine became a Christian, naturally the Christians could come up out of the catacombs and worship aboveground. The Christians found that the best kind of aboveground buildings for their worship services were the basilicas. You remember that basilicas were the buildings built by the Romans for courthouses. In the courthouses the judge sat in the middle at one end, with his back toward the end wall. In front of the judge was a long aisle with columns on each side; this aisle led to the front door. On each side of the main aisle was another aisle. Look at our illustration of a floor plan of a basilica. The lines are the walls and the dots are the columns. The place where the judge sat is the half circle at the top of the plan.

The Christians used the judge's half circle in their basilica church for an altar and for the priest to preach from. This part of the building had lattice-work railings in front of it called *cancelli* by the Romans. That's why some churches still call that end of the church the *chancel*. The people who came to worship in the basilica sat on benches facing the chancel—just as they do in some churches today. The main central part of a church is called a *nave*. The chancel and the aisles on the side are not part of the nave.

The windows in a basilica were way up near the roof. The center part, or nave, was higher than the side aisles and so the roof over the center part was higher than the roof over the side aisles. The nave was really two stories high and the side aisles only one story high. The windows were in the second story of the nave. The part with the windows was called the *clerestory*, which means clear story. I think you can guess why it is called that.

From the outside, these basilicas weren't much to look at. Many of them looked more like big barns than anything else. But inside they were magnificently decorated. The columns were beautiful marble ones taken from older buildings. The walls had mosaic pictures on them made of little pieces of stone or of colored glass which shone like jewels. The floors and lower walls were covered with fine slabs of marble. After the catacombs they must have seemed all the more magnificent to the early Christians.

The largest of these early Christian basilicas is the church of St. Paul Outside the Walls. The name means that the Basilica of St. Paul is outside the wall of Rome. It has a main part, or nave, and *two* aisles on each side instead of one on each side. Our illustration shows the inside of the nave looking toward the chancel. You can see the clerestory windows very plainly. St. Paul Outside the Walls was built in 380 A.D. People worshiped there for more than 1400 years, until in 1823 it caught fire and burned to the ground. But it was rebuilt the way it was before the fire, and can still be visited in Rome.

opposite above: Exterior view of the Basilica of St. Paul Outside the Walls, Rome

---

opposite below: Interior view of the Basilica of St. Paul Outside the Walls, Rome

Alinari-Art Reference Bureau

Alinari-Art Reference Bureau

Byzantine Architecture

Men of one part of a country speak differently from men of another part. Men from different countries are different in other ways. They wear different kinds of clothes, they have different kinds of laws, they eat different kinds of food, they paint different kinds of pictures, they build different kinds of buildings.

When the Roman emperor Constantine became a Christian, the Christians in Rome came out of the catacombs and built basilicas for churches. But other Christians who lived a long way from Rome were subject to the Roman emperor. The Roman Empire reached eastward into Asia. Many people in this eastern part of the empire were Christians, too. Under Constantine they began to build churches just as the Christians in Rome did. But, because they belonged to a different part of the world, the eastern Christians built their churches in their own way. They didn't care much for basilicas.

Eastern Christian architecture was called Byzantine, because Byzantium was the largest city in the eastern part of the Roman Empire. The city is still a large and important city, but you won't find Byzantium on the map. The name was changed when Constantine went to live in Byzantium and made it his capital instead of Rome. When he did this he named the city Constantinople, or City of Constantine. But you won't find Constantinople on the modern map, either, for now it is called Istanbul. The word Byzantine, however, is still used to describe the architecture that began to be used there.

There was one very important difference between this Byzantine architecture and the basilican architecture. A Byzantine church always had some kind of dome on it. In some churches the dome was small; in some it was covered with a square roof so the dome could be seen only from below, on the inside; in many churches there were several domes.

The Pantheon in Rome has a dome, but the Pantheon is not like the Byzantine style of building. The Pantheon's dome is made of concrete. The domes of Byzantine churches usually were made of bricks or tiles. The Pantheon dome rests on a circular wall. The Byzantine domes cover a square space.

The plan of most Byzantine churches looks like this: + This kind of cross, with all the arms equal, is called a Greek cross. The central dome was usually right over the square in the center of the cross.

Historical Pictures Service, Chicago

Office of the Turkish Press Counselor, Washington, D.C.

All these Byzantine buildings with domes were quite small until the Emperor Justinian came to rule. Justinian had his architects build the best and finest and biggest building ever built in the Byzantine style. Most people call it St. Sophia or Santa Sofia, but Sofia was not the name of any saint. *Sofia* means wisdom and the real name of Justinian's church is *Hagia Sophia,* or Holy Wisdom.

In the middle of St. Sophia is a huge dome. This dome rests on the top of four big arches that are shaped like croquet wickets. Each arch stands on one side of a square.

The bottom of the dome rests on the tops of these arches.

The spaces between the arches below the dome are filled in with brick so the bottom of the dome is resting on something all the way around. These spaces between the tops of the arches look like curved triangles pointed downward. The curved triangles are called *pendentives.* It is the use of pendentives that makes Byzantine architecture very different from other kinds of architecture. You won't find any pendentives in the Pantheon in Rome, for instance.

Our illustration on the next page shows three of the arches under the dome and two of the pendentives between the arches.

Since the dome of St. Sophia is made of bricks, the whole dome isn't held together like a saucer or like the concrete Pantheon dome. This means that the brick dome pushes down on the walls that hold it up, and also pushes outward or sideways on the walls. You know how a ladder leaning against the wall of a room will slide out at the bottom when a heavy man climbs the ladder unless the bottom is braced against something on the floor. Well, the domes pushes out in *all* directions just as the ladder goes in *one* direction, so there must be something to brace the walls to keep the dome from pushing them over.

opposite above: Exterior view of St. Sophia, Istanbul (formerly Constantinople)

---

opposite below: Interior detail of St. Sophia, Istanbul

Historical Pictures Service, Chicago

The arches resting on the ground hold the downward push of the dome. The architects of St. Sophia took care of the outward push very cleverly. On the outside of two arches that are opposite each other, they built half domes on walls reaching to the ground. These half domes brace the two arches just like bookends pushing toward the middle of the building. They are props to keep the arches from falling outward.

Against the legs of the other two arches they built big piles of stone and brick called *buttresses.* These buttresses keep the arches in place just like bookends, too.

And then—after all this care and work—the dome of St. Sophia fell down! It collapsed a few years after it was finished. But we can't blame the architects or the builders. An earthquake shook the bricks out of place and down came the dome.

When the dome was put up again an improvement was made. All around the bottom of the new dome little windows were made—forty windows altogether. This let in such a band of light that the dome seems to be resting on light when you look up at it from inside, or as if it were hanging from the sky a few feet above the top of the four big arches.

The inside of St. Sophia has been called the most magnificent interior in the world. Along each side of the nave run aisles which have second stories or galleries. The galleries are supported by many columns of different-colored marbles, some red, some green, some gray or black. There are 107 columns inside the building and the dome is just 107 feet across from one side to the other.

---

opposite: Interior of St. Sophia, Istanbul

The lower walls are all covered with slabs of beautiful marble, in even more colors than the columns. Higher up on the walls are mosaic pictures in which the pieces of colored glass and marble are set in gold.

Almost a thousand years after the church of St. Sophia was built, Constantinople was captured by the Turks. The Turks are Mohammedans instead of Christians, and worship in mosques instead of churches. The leader of the Turks rode his horse right into St. Sophia and ordered the Christian church turned into a Mohammedan mosque. The beautiful Christian mosaics were covered with plaster and whitewash except for a few of the angels. And until recently no one has been allowed to enter St. Sophia without first taking off his shoes. That is the rule for all mosques. No shoes may tread on Mohammed's holy ground. St. Sophia is no longer a mosque. The Turks recently decided to turn it into a museum and are now uncovering all the Christian mosaics that they once covered with plaster!

From the outside St. Sophia looks big, but some people think it is not very beautiful. Notice in the picture the great buttresses that stick up on each side of the arch to brace the push of the dome.

The towers you see in the picture were not part of the original church, but were put on by the Turks when the church became a mosque.

I don't want you to believe that St. Sophia was the only great Byzantine building or that all Byzantine buildings were in Constantinople. The Byzantine style of architecture spread wherever the religion of the Greek Christian Church spread. The churches of Russia, for instance, were almost all built in the Byzantine style because the Russians became members of the Greek Church instead of members of the Roman Church. Churches in the Byzantine style are still being built in many parts of the world.

---

opposite: St. Basil's, Moscow

KLM Royal Dutch Airlines News Service

Photograph by Ente Provinciale per il Turismo—Venice

Just as famous as St. Sophia is another Byzantine church built in Venice, hundreds of years after St. Sophia was built. Venice was a seaport republic. The city belonged to no country. It was independent. Fleets of ships from Venice sailed away to the East and brought back the beautiful silks and spices of Asia. Venice became rich and powerful. Her people learned to love the bright colors of the goods from the East and they put so much lovely color on their Byzantine church that it shone like a beautiful jewel in the sun. They called their church St. Mark's because it was built over the spot where Saint Mark was supposed to lie buried.

St. Mark's has five domes—a big dome in the center and four smaller domes around it. The domes were not high enough to be seen well on the outside, so the Venetians made a much higher dome over each of the five domes. So each dome is double. The Church is covered inside and out with brilliant mosaics and slabs of precious alabaster brought from far and near. The four bronze horses over the main door are almost as famous as the church itself. It is one of the most colorful buildings in the world.

---

opposite: St. Mark's, Venice

Christian Monasteries in the Dark Ages

"What goes up must come down." The Roman Empire had reached the height of its power. The Romans had conquered, ruled, and civilized almost all of Europe. Then the mighty empire that the Romans had built up came tumbling down.

It began with the split between the eastern part of the empire and the western. When the capital was moved to Constantinople, naturally Rome, the old capital, lost power. Finally the East and West separated. Constantinople remained the capital of the Eastern Roman Empire. Rome was capital of the Western Roman Empire. So then there were two Roman Empires and two emperors. But this didn't last long.

Barbaric men from the North began pushing and fighting their way down across France to Italy. These men were fierce and rough. They had never learned to read or write. We call them Teutons. The Teutons finally overran France, Spain, and Italy. They took Rome itself, and that ended the old Roman Empire in the West.

The Teutons were rude and rough and ignorant. But they were strong and brave and good fighters. They became

Christians. Gradually they learned the languages of the parts of Europe where they settled. All parts of the Roman Empire had at one time spoken Latin, the language of Rome. Now under the Teuton tribes the language of each part of Europe became different. The Latin used in France gradually became French. The Latin used in Spain became Spanish, and the Latin used in Italy and in Rome itself became Italian. No longer could a man from Spain talk with a man from France in his own language.

But Spain and France and Italy did not become real nations right away. Everywhere there was fighting, everywhere mix-ups. One tribe fought with another. One town fought with another town. The old civilized life was upset. Everything became darker and darker for civilization. The ways of the Romans were forgotten. There would have been no time for architecture, because so much time was spent fighting. The old basilican churches were still used, but few new ones were built. Things got so bad that we call the time from about 500 A.D. to about 1000 A.D. the Dark Ages.

At this time, although everything certainly looked black for Europe, there *were* a few lights to be seen in the darkness. One bright spot was the reign of Charlemagne. Charlemagne was a Teuton. He grew up uneducated and he never learned to write. But Charlemagne had a good mind and he wanted to learn all there was to know. He became king of France, but he wasn't satisfied until he had brought Germany and Italy under his rule, too.

Charlemagne encouraged building. He brought to his court all the wisest men he could find. He helped to recover for the world some of the knowledge and learning that had been lost when the old Romans ceased to govern. He was crowned emperor of a new Roman Empire in 800 A.D.

Another light that flickered in the Dark Ages was kept burning by the Christian monks. As you know, monks are men who live in monasteries. A monastery was ruled by a monk called an abbot. The monks thought they could live better lives if they worked hard and kept away from all the fighting in the world around them.

Those monks worked hard in the monasteries. They raised vegetables, built churches and houses, taught school, made paintings, wrote histories, and helped the poor people who came to them. Best of all for you and me, they studied the old Roman writings and kept them safe. Today we know much more about the old Roman ways than we could have if it hadn't been for the learned monks.

---

opposite: Monastery Maria Stella at Wettingen

Historical Pictures Service, Chicago

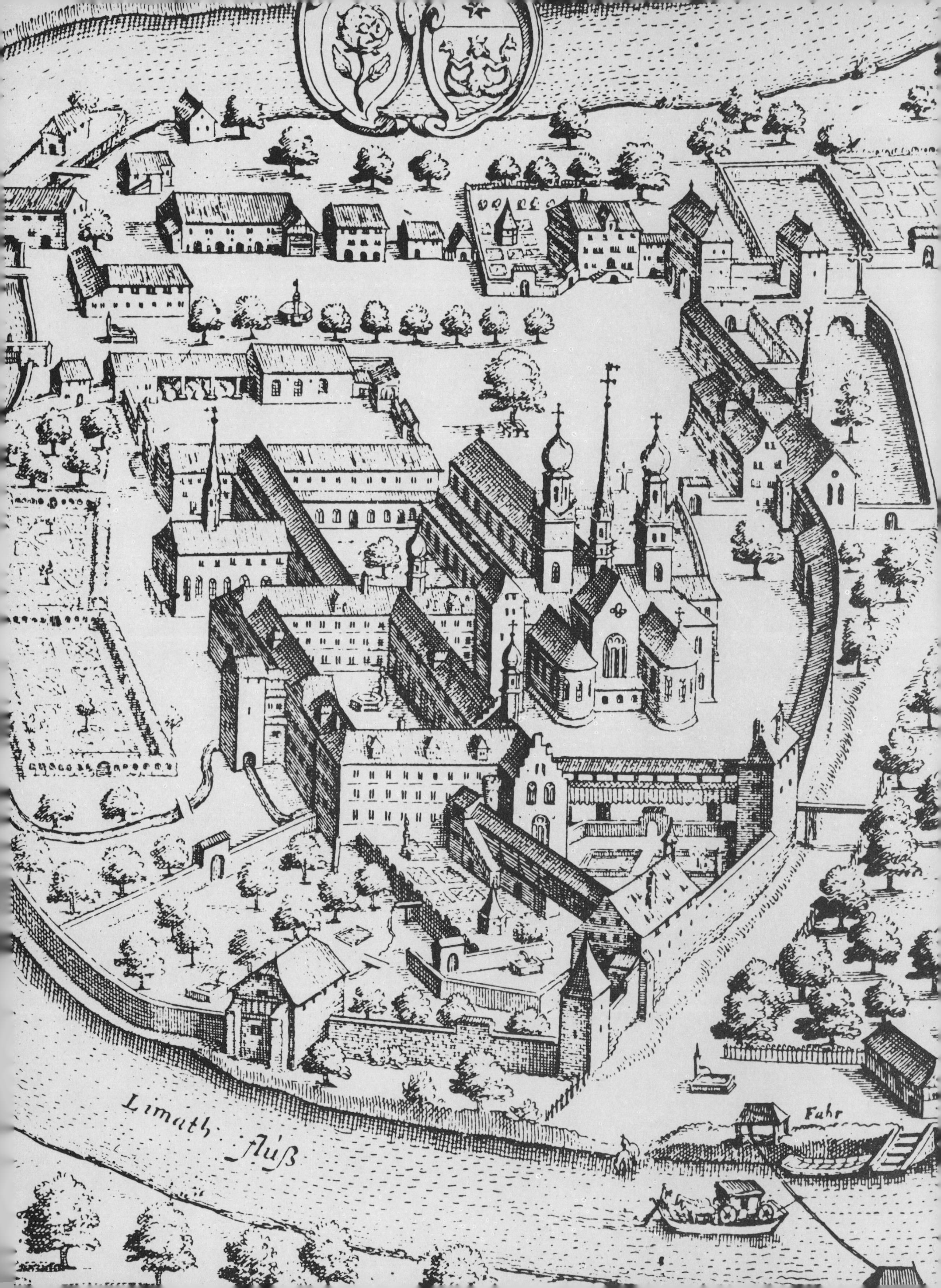
Limath flüß
Fahr

The monastery that the monks lived in was built around a church. Such a church was called an *abbey* because an abbot ruled the monastery. On one side of the abbey was a courtyard. Across the courtyard from the church was usually the dining hall, which was called the *refectory.* The church and the refectory were connected along each end of the courtyard by hallways. These hallways were like long porches with columns on the sides facing the courtyard, and were called *cloisters.* The columns in the cloisters were not like the old Greek and Roman columns. They weren't Doric or Ionic or Corinthian or Tuscan or Composite, but were of many different shapes, even in the same cloister. Some were twisted in shape like a screw. Some were decorated with bands around them or with crisscross stripes. In many cloisters the columns were in pairs, two and two, like animals going into Noah's ark. These were called *coupled columns.*

---

opposite: Cloisters at the Basilica of St. Paul Outside the Walls, Rome

Photograph by Ente Provinciale per il Turismo—Rome

Romanesque Architecture

Suppose you thought the world were going to end next year! Most people in Europe in the Dark Ages thought the world was going to come to an end in 1000 A.D. They weren't sure just how it would happen. They thought that perhaps it was going to burn up or fall apart or blow up with earthquakes and volcanoes. But they felt sure from what they read in the Bible that in 1000 A.D. the world was going to come to an end. Important buildings were not built, because what was the use? They'd all be destroyed with the end of the world.

Then 1000 A.D. came and nothing happened to the world. Still the world was there, and people discovered that they must have been mistaken. They began building more good buildings. The light in the darkness of the Dark Ages began to get brighter.

The kind of architecture that was used after 1000 A.D. is called Romanesque. The easiest way to tell that a building is Romanesque is to look at the tops of the windows and doors. If all the windows and doors have round arches for tops, then the building is probably Romanesque.

It is called Romanesque because it was used in the countries that once belonged to Rome. Just as each of these former Roman countries came to have its own language, descended from Latin, so each country came to have its own Romanesque architecture, descended from Roman architecture.

The Romanesque architecture of Italy is most like the old basilican kind, so I'll tell you first about the most famous Italian Romanesque buildings.

I'm sure you know of the famous Leaning Tower of Pisa. The building next to the tower is the cathedral. Every church isn't a cathedral. A cathedral is a church with a

opposite: Aerial view of Pisa

bishop. The chair that the bishop used in his church was called a *cathedra*. Because the bishop's church always had a cathedra, the bishop's church was called a cathedral. This was the cathedral of the Bishop of Pisa.

If you were to look down on a cathedral from an airplane you would see that it was built in the shape of a cross. But this cross isn't a Greek cross, because all the arms are not the same length. A cross with the main stem longer than the other parts is called a Latin cross. Most Romanesque churches were built in the form of a Latin cross. The top of the cross was always pointed toward the east so that the altar in that end of the church could be nearer Palestine in the East, where Christ was born.

The outside of the cathedral at Pisa is worth looking at carefully. The rows of columns with arches over them are called arcades. All the arches are round arches, which is one way to tell that the building is probably Romanesque. There are four of these rows of arches or arcades on the west end of this cathedral.

Each arcade is a different height. The third arcade from the ground has the tallest columns. The arcade next to the bottom is not quite as tall, the top one is still shorter, and the bottom arcade has the shortest columns of all. The middle arch in the two arcades nearest the ground is bigger than the other arches. The columns in the two top arcades are not always exactly over the columns below them.

All these differences were not just accidental. The arcades were built that way on purpose. If all four arcades had been just alike they would have made the whole front of the cathedral look tiresome, monotonous, uninteresting.

---

opposite: Leaning Tower and Cathedral, Pisa

Sabena Belgian World Airlines

Italian State Tourist Office-Enit. Foto Enit-Roma.

If you will look at the Leaning Tower, you can see that all the arcades *are* just alike. For that reason, the tower isn't as beautiful as the cathedral. Many people think the tower is ugly. I don't think it is ugly, but I certainly can't say it's as pleasing to look at as the cathedral. You may find it more interesting, however, because of the way it leans. The Leaning Tower was built later than the cathedral. Maybe by then the architects had forgotten why the cathedral arcades were not built all alike.

The tower started leaning almost as soon as it was begun. Before the first story was finished, the foundations on one side were much lower than on the other, so work on the building was stopped. But, after several years, another architect managed to get three more stories built before he had to stop because of the slant. Still later another architect finished the tower. Some people have said that the tower was meant to lean in the first place so that it would be different from other towers.

It is true that each city in Italy was trying to get ahead of every other city with buildings that would attract attention. But most people now believe that the foundations sank in soft ground on one side and that the lean of the tower was an accident. The top of the tower leans about fourteen feet out over the bottom. There are seven bells in the top and the heaviest bell is kept on the side away from the lean to help balance the tower.

Near the cathedral stands a circular building called the Baptistery of Pisa. The Baptistery was the building in which people were baptized. It was changed a great deal in looks after the Romanesque period was over, because later architects tried to make it look better than it did at first.

left:
Baptistery, Pisa

A good example of a Romanesque building in France is the Cathedral of Angoulême. The front is decorated with sculpture. Notice the round arches that all Romanesque buildings have.

In England, the Normans who came over with William the Conqueror built many stone churches, cathedrals, and castles. Norman buildings are just as much Romanesque as the French and Italian, but the architecture is usually called Norman rather than Romanesque. Very little of the Norman Romanesque looks now as it did when the Normans built it, because later builders kept adding to it and changing it. Often some parts of an English church are Norman, while later parts of the same church are not in the Norman style.

Germany also has some fine Romanesque cathedrals and churches—and they all have arcades and round arches over the windows and doors. That's really the most important thing to remember about Romanesque buildings—round arches and arcades.

---

opposite: Angoulême Cathedral

French Embassy Press and Information Division, New York

Castles in the Middle Ages

In the Middle Ages there were many castles—most of them built on the top of a hill. These castles were built because of the *feudal system*. The feudal system worked like this: The king or prince who conquered a country would divide the country among several of his lords. These lords would then divide their parts of the land among other lords, and these lords would divide their share again among the knights. Each lord and knight had to promise that he would help the lord from whom he got his land whenever the lord needed him. Then each lord and knight built himself a strong castle to protect his part of the land from anyone who might try to take it away from him. Each knight had to have his own soldiers and his own castle to protect his land and his rights.

Common people called *serfs* worked the land for the knights. Most of these people had to give part of all the food they raised to the lord of the castle, and all the men had to serve the lord as soldiers whenever he needed them. In return, the lord of the castle protected them from enemies.

The castle was built with great, thick stone walls all around it. Outside of the wall was a deep ditch of water called a *moat*. The only way to get into the castle was to cross a drawbridge over the moat. The drawbridge could be drawn up from inside the castle so that an enemy could not enter. If the enemy reached the drawbridge before it was drawn up, he found his way blocked by a huge latticework gate, called a *portcullis*, which was dropped across the gatepost of the castle.

left: A German fortress with moat

Historical Pictures Service, Chicago

overleaf: Chateau de Pierrefonds (Oise)

French Embassy Press and Information Division, New York

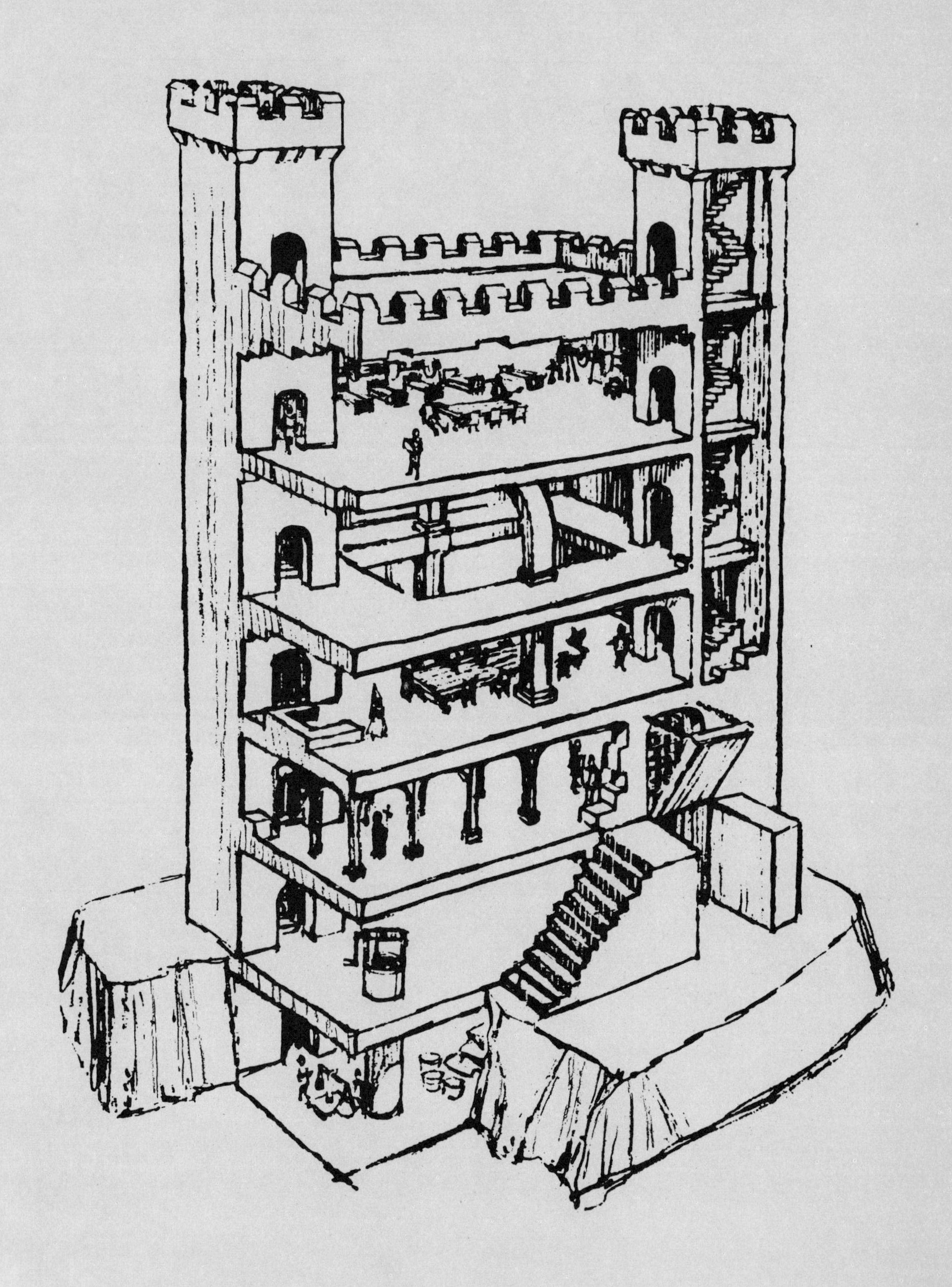

The castle had huge stone towers at the gateway and along the wall, with very narrow slits for windows. Archers could shoot arrows out of these slits, but it was hard to shoot through the slits from the outside.

Inside the walls there was a courtyard around which were the stables, soldiers' and servants' quarters, kitchens, and a high tower called the *keep*. The lord of the castle lived in the keep. There was a large dining hall and often a little church or chapel in the keep. Down below the ground level were prison cells and torture chambers. In case of an attack, all the people who lived on the lord's lands came into the castle, often with their cattle and flocks, and stayed there. This made it necessary for great stores of food to be kept on hand.

---

opposite: Cross section of a keep

German Tourist Information Office, Chicago

Burg Katz on the Rhine River

Historical Pictures Service, Chicago

above: The lord's chamber in a twelfth-century castle

right: Siege of a fifteenth-century castle by men with cannon and crossbows

You have learned much about architecture in this book, but this is only the beginning! Some of the most interesting and exciting ideas in architecture came much later than the times we have been discussing here.

So much happened after these times that we have used a whole book to tell you about it. I'm sure you will be interested in reading about magnificent Gothic cathedrals, towering skyscrapers and buildings made all of steel and glass.

Historical Pictures Service, Chicago

INDEX: Young People's Story of Architecture, 3000 B.C. to Gothic Period

Type *Century Expanded*
Typesetter *American Typesetting Corporation*
Printer *The Regensteiner Corporation*